Getting Work Done

20 MINUTE MANAGER SERIES

Get up to speed fast on essential business skills. Whether you're looking for a crash course or a brief refresher, you'll find just what you need in HBR's 20-Minute Manager series—foundational reading for ambitious professionals and aspiring executives. Each book is a concise, practical primer, so you'll have time to brush up on a variety of key management topics.

Advice you can quickly read and apply, from the most trusted source in business.

Titles include:

Creating Business Plans

Delegating Work

Finance Basics

Getting Work Done

Giving Effective Feedback

Innovative Teams

Managing Projects

Managing Time

Managing Up

Performance Reviews

Presentations

Running Meetings

20 MINUTE MANAGER SERIES

Getting Work Done

Prioritize your work
Be more efficient
Take control of your time

HARVARD BUSINESS REVIEW PRESS

Boston, Massachusetts

Library of Congress Cataloging-in-Publication Data

Getting work done : prioritize your work, be more efficient, take control of your time.
    pages cm. — (20-minute manager series)
  Includes index.
  ISBN 978-1-62527-543-1 (alk. paper)
  1. Time management.   2. Labor productivity.   3. Performance.
4. Orderliness.
  HD69.T54G48 2014
  650.1'1—dc23

                                                    2014021084

ISBN: 9781625275431
eISBN: 9781625275486

Preview

Demands on your time are growing by the hour, and work keeps piling up. Unclear goals, constant interruptions, and urgent tasks are competing for your attention; you know that you're working less effectively than you could be. This book will teach you how to become more focused and organized at work so you can be more productive by showing you how to:

- Prioritize your tasks

- Create to-do lists that work

- Organize your physical and virtual workspace

- Develop a daily routine and stick to it

Preview

- Stay focused and stop procrastinating

- Work more efficiently with others

- Assess your progress

Contents

Contents

Getting Work Done

Why Invest Time in Improving Your Productivity?

Why Invest Time in Improving Your Productivity?

D o you feel so swamped with work that you don't know where to start? Though you know that it's essential to work efficiently to ensure that you get everything done, these feelings can be paralyzing and cause you to spiral into a panic that actually makes you less productive. How do you get out of this cycle and get started?

This book will begin by highlighting the basics of time management: how to track, prioritize, and log your work so you can see where inefficiencies lie and where your goals aren't being met. It will then show you how to schedule your tasks and create helpful to-do lists, organize the virtual and physical space around you in order to achieve better focus, train yourself in better habits and routines, and work more effectively with others.

Your first reaction may be to rebel against these efforts. Your time is already sapped; why would you expend more of it making lists, planning and executing changes to your work habits, and tracking your progress? Though improving your productivity requires time and effort up front, you will get more accomplished in the long run—and you'll do it more deliberately and calmly. By tracking your time, you'll discover inefficiencies that will help you identify tasks that should be prioritized or delegated; by getting more organized, you will clear away distractions so you can stop procrastinating and finally focus; by adjusting your work habits and establishing new routines, you will discover newfound energy to put toward the work that matters; and by assessing your progress over time, you'll be able to adjust how you're working as your goals evolve.

Commit to change

It's important to believe that you *can* become more organized, that you can change your work habits and improve your efficiency. You may think that you're built to work a certain way or that the way you work is too ingrained to be altered—either you're a morning person or you're not; either you're organized or you thrive in chaos and clutter. This is not true. Good habits can be learned, and, even better, they can become routine.

In today's world of instant communication, we have become drawn to urgency. It pulls us in and gives us a false sense of productivity (see the sidebar "Busy Doesn't Mean Productive"). But putting systems in place to organize your work helps to dissipate the stress and lets you work with more forethought, focus, and energy. Most importantly, it will give you time and attention for your most important work, the

BUSY DOESN'T MEAN PRODUCTIVE

Do you find yourself running from meeting to meeting, dashing off responses to e-mails while zipping through the halls, and focusing on routine tasks in order to feel a sense of accomplishment? If so, you may not be as productive as you think.

It's time to take stock of your work and your priorities. Busyness can be a dangerous way to make up for a lack of purpose or a feeling that you aren't a good fit within a particular role or organization. You can schedule your day in an attempt to make yourself, and others, see value in you, but being busy may prevent you from reaching your true potential. Admit to yourself that it might be time to improve the way you work.

work that actually contributes to your personal goals and those your organization has set for you.

In order to truly understand what work is most important and how to become more efficient, you need to first identify your goals and recognize how you're currently spending your time. We'll start there.

Identify What Needs to Get Done

Identify What Needs to Get Done

What goals are you aiming for in your work? Does the way that you are spending your time actually correlate to those goals? Without answers to these questions, you won't know how the many tasks on your list should be prioritized, organized, and ultimately accomplished.

List your goals

Ideally, you and your manager should meet at the start of each year to formulate a set of performance goals. From your discussion, you should understand how those goals tie into the company's aims and mission. You likely also have your own personal career goals. Together, these may look something like, "Improve people-management skills. Manage six new products. Handle contracts for all of the department's new products. Develop vendor-management skills."

Revisiting them now, write these goals down—on paper or in a note-taking app if you prefer. You will use these goals in two ways: first, to prioritize your daily work; and second, to gauge your progress (in other words, to benchmark what you're accomplishing and whether the changes you make as a result of this book are effective for you). By referring back to this list regularly, you'll be able to identify which tasks are most important for you to tackle so you can plan accordingly.

Track your time

Once you've identified your goals, it's time to examine how you're currently spending your time. Are you working on the things you *should* be doing—the things that will allow you to reach those goals—or are you getting bogged down by unrelated tasks or unexpected crises?

In order to truly understand where you are spending your time and to identify whether you should adjust your workload, track your work for two weeks by completing the following exercise. You may discover that your results don't align with your goals. The point is to uncover where that misalignment occurs so you can correct it.

First, write down your activities. Consider this a brain dump, and leave no stone unturned. List all of the tasks you perform, meetings you attend, and even the time you spend socializing or procrastinating at work. It can help to look back over your calendar for the last week or two to get a sense of your range of activities. Once you have a full list, break it down into broad categories so you can track the amount of time you spend doing tasks in each category. Some categories to consider include:

- *Core responsibilities:* day-to-day tasks that make up the crux of your job.

- *Personal growth:* activities and projects that you find meaningful and valuable, but may not be part of your everyday responsibilities.

- *Managing people:* your work with others, including direct reports, colleagues, and even your superiors.

- *Crises and fires:* interruptions and urgent matters that arise occasionally and unexpectedly.

- *Free time:* lunch breaks and time spent writing personal e-mails, browsing the web, or checking social media.

- *Administrative tasks:* necessary tasks that you perform each day, such as approving time sheets or invoices, or putting together expense reports.

Seeing your work broken into categories like this will help you visualize how you're really spending your time, and you may already be getting a sense of whether this lines up with the goals you identified.

Then, track your time. Once you have your categories established, begin tracking how much time you spend doing tasks in each. You can estimate by the hour, or if you want to dig deeper into your habits, you can get more granular. To record your results, use either an online time-tracking tool or a standard calendar; to analyze those results, use a spreadsheet like the one depicted in table 1. List each category in its own column, and write the days of the week in each row. Calculate the time you spend on each task for each category for the next two weeks and put the totals in the corresponding categories.

TABLE 1

Time-tracking tool

Week ending 4/14	Core responsibilities	Personal growth	Managing people	Crises and fires	Free time	Administrative tasks	Total time/day
Monday	2 hrs	1 hr	3 hrs	0 hrs	0 hrs	2 hrs	8 hrs
Tuesday	3	1	4	0	0	2	10
Wednesday	7	0	0	1	0	2	10
Thursday	0	3	3	0	0	2	8
Friday	1	2	0	1	3	2	9
Total time/activity	13 hrs	7 hrs	10 hrs	2 hrs	3 hrs	10 hrs	45 hrs
% of time	29%	16%	22%	4%	7%	22%	100%

At this point, you may be thinking, I'm busy; I don't have time to log everything I do. It's true: This system does require an up-front investment of time and effort.

But logging your tasks and how long it takes to complete them will let you clearly see where you're spending too much time and where you need to begin to reallocate time to achieve your goals. If you want to improve your people management skills, for example, you may realize that devoting 10 hours a week is not enough; perhaps you need to offload some administrative tasks so you have the additional time you need for that goal. By making small, deliberate shifts in how you spend your day, you'll ensure that you're investing the right amount of time on the tasks that matter most, making you more efficient at achieving your goals.

Schedule
Your Work

Schedule Your Work

N ow that you know what your goals are and have identified where you may need to be spending more or less time, it's time to tackle your task list—all those competing priorities, projects, and activities that you need to do in the near future. First, identify the most important work you need to do; then figure out when to do it.

Set priorities

Go through your task list—everything you need to do that you have marked down on sticky notes, in notebooks, or in e-mail reminders to yourself—and determine what is most important and what is most urgent.

Without a clear way to identify the important work from the not so important, you're likely to treat every item on your list and request that comes your way as urgent. But "urgent" and "important" are different. By staying focused on the goals you identified, you can separate out what *seems* urgent but really isn't.

E-mails in which the sender demands an immediate response (but without a specific reason), projects that seem quick but turn out to be more involved, and simple tasks that are just more appealing than other work you need to do—these activities often present themselves as pressing even if they are not.

Resist the temptation to get drawn into these tasks without thinking them through. Some cases—a request from your boss with a tight deadline—might actually require your immediate attention. Others may be able to wait until after you've completed your more important work. Evaluate each item on your task list based on its importance—how closely it aligns with the goals you've identified and the way you want to spend your time—and its true urgency based on the following four descriptions, first defined by productivity expert Stephen Covey.

1. *Urgent and important.* These are the crises and deadlines that you need to address—a problem with a product that you oversee, the website that you help to maintain, or a big client that you handle, for example. These should always be your highest priority.

2. *Not urgent but important.* These tasks have a high impact on you or your organization, but aren't necessarily time sensitive. They are likely to be closely related to your goals: acquisition of a new skill or work on a big project, for example. Because they're not urgent, you might fail to devote enough time to them, which is why you should make them your second priority.

3. *Urgent but less important.* These tasks need to be done quickly, but have a lower impact if they're finished late or if they're never done at all. When considering whether something is less important, be sure to consider its potential impact not only on you but on your group or organization as well. These should be your third priority.

4. *Not urgent and less important.* These are the tasks that don't require immediate attention and aren't urgent. These should be your last priority. (See the section "Learn to Say No" later in the book for more on recognizing when you shouldn't agree to take on new tasks suggested by colleagues.)

By prioritizing your tasks in this way, you can identify what needs to happen first and what can be put off until later. This will help as you begin to set real deadlines for your work and decide when you will do which tasks.

You'll also begin to see what work you can actually handle and what you can—and should—delegate to others. (See the section "Delegate" later in this book.) Lowest-priority items are often those that can often be handed off. This is the fastest path to obtaining additional time that you can use toward more important work.

Use deadlines to your advantage

Now that you have a sense of which tasks are most important and need to be done first (or last), it's time to think about when to actually do them.

When planning any kind of project (even one without a prescribed deadline), set realistic, meaningful end dates. Deadlines put pressure on everyone involved, but they are also crucial to get a project moving. Some of your tasks may have a deadline already assigned—a report that's due at noon on Friday, for example. But for others, you shouldn't be afraid to set your own deadlines and to commit to them according to the priorities you set earlier.

When setting a deadline, break the project down into manageable tasks and record how long each step should take. This will help to ensure that you've allotted the appropriate amount of time to each task. Consider how long it has taken to complete a similar task in the past, think about what might not go as planned, and allot time in the schedule to change course if needed. If the project is new to you, seek advice from someone who has worked on a similar project. Could you share your estimates with your manager for her feedback? Are you working with another colleague or an external vendor who could help you gauge appropriate timing? Making these inquiries in advance will ensure that the time you're allocating to each task is realistic.

Breaking a larger project into its component parts with individual due dates will guarantee that you have budgeted time for each part of the process, and these interim deadlines will also help you avoid leaving the bulk of the project to the last minute. You will feel a sense of accomplishment as you complete each piece according to your schedule, and you'll avoid that overwhelming panic that consumes you when you leave something until the eleventh hour.

While deadlines can facilitate getting work done in a timely manner, they can bring their own pressures and frustrations. Deadlines can take a toll if they are unrealistic, so make every effort to avoid the extreme pressure that comes from not allotting adequate time to specific tasks. Especially if you need to explore new ideas or think creatively, give yourself the time you'll need.

That said, it's tempting to give yourself extra time to avoid additional pressure, but artificially extending deadlines doesn't work. When you do this, you lose motivation, you procrastinate, and you don't leave yourself time to react if something doesn't go as planned. Once you set a deadline, keep to it. Extending a deadline just for the sake of granting yourself an extension will have a cascading effect on the rest of your schedule. Put in the work up front to create a realistic schedule and then follow it.

Add the deadlines for each task to your calendar. Even if you have them all in one place in a separate project plan, for example, it's still helpful to be reminded of them on a day-to-day basis; you'll see at a glance if you're overscheduled, and you'll be reminded of upcoming milestones as they approach.

Schedule your tasks

Now that you know what work has to get done and you've assigned deadlines for completion, you need to decide when you'll actually do the work. You should consider this regularly—at the beginning of each week, for example, but also daily as you arrive in the morning or before you go home, to take into account new tasks and what you accomplished that day.

Looking at each of the deadlines you've set and your calendar, plot out what work you're going to do when—you'll write marketing copy at 3 p.m. on Wednesday, for example. Recording these activities directly on your calendar will help you see quickly if all of your tasks are achievable within the time frame you have to complete them. Projects will also feel less daunting if they are spread out and assigned to specific days.

When scheduling your time:

- Put your most demanding and important tasks at the beginning of the day. This is when you're fresh and energized, and haven't yet been interrupted by other workplace demands. Tackle those tough tasks first, and you'll feel a sense of accomplishment that will enable you to complete the less onerous tasks around the other commitments of your day.

- Similarly, keep in mind your energy levels throughout the day. Schedule easy tasks between harder ones to reward yourself for getting the tough ones done and to give yourself a mental break.

- If you have several similar tasks to get done in a week, try grouping them together—do all of your travel reports or invoicing during one hour-long chunk, for example. Checking these tasks off as a group is rewarding and helps you hit those deadlines easily. It also minimizes switching back and forth between different kinds of tasks, which can erode your efficiency.

As you add your tasks into your calendar, you'll quickly realize that there aren't enough hours in the day to achieve everything you'd like. This exercise forces you to prioritize your most important tasks and to schedule those that are less important into time slots on another day.

But in some cases, you may still have items on your list that haven't made it onto your calendar, tasks you seem to carry over every day, or every week, and you never seem to get to. Sometimes these are administrative in nature, such as creating a new filing system to store vendor contracts, or they're related to longer-term goals, such as brainstorming ideas for a new product. Take a moment to review these tasks and decide what to do with each one:

1. *Just do it now.* Wouldn't it feel great to cross that task off your list, even if it never does bubble up to top priority? If that's the case, just do it and move on. Respond to that voice mail, cancel that meeting, or book that flight. Then move on to more important work.

2. *Schedule the task for later.* You've determined the task doesn't require immediate attention, you can't check it off quickly, but it still needs to get done. Slot it on your calendar for a later

date and adjust any related deadlines accordingly. It won't get done if you don't schedule it, and even if that means you put it on your calendar for a month from now, get it on there. You can reconsider it when that day comes.

3. *Remove the task.* If you aren't willing to complete the task or schedule it, this could mean that you're never going to get to it. This is a clear signal that whatever it is, it is not a priority. Admit this to yourself, talk to your manager, and get permission to remove the task from your list, either by delegating it or deciding together that it's just not going to happen.

You've now organized and prioritized your tasks and removed those tasks that you do not have time to get done. Now it's time to create your to-do list.

Create your daily to-do list

As the last step in this process, look at your calendar. What do you need to do today? If you've already scheduled time for each task on your calendar, making the day's to-do list should be rather straightforward. There are two keys to employing to-do lists successfully.

First, break down your tasks. A to-do is one single task that will move a project or goal forward. (This concept should be familiar from what you did to break down your deadlines.) For example, if your task is to create a production schedule for a catalog, one to-do is to e-mail the print vendor and set a print date that will allow you to create that schedule. Going through the exercise of creating a to-do list also reminds you of each step that needs to happen toward achieving your tasks in a given day.

Second, be specific. Don't leave yourself cryptic notes. You might have "Schedule lunch with Elsa" on your to-do list, but by the time you get to that item, you forget what the purpose of the lunch was or when you wanted to schedule it. Be more specific so that it's clear why your to-do is important. Write it all out: "Schedule lunch with Elsa on Friday at 1 p.m. to discuss the upcoming client meeting."

To create your actual physical list:

1. *Put your list on a note card or oblong sheet of paper.* Create a list you can see and carry with you. By putting it on a sheet of paper that is a special shape or size, it will stand out from the other papers on your desk.

2. *Note the due date next to the task.* This is yet another reminder of how much time you have.

3. *Highlight your top priorities.* Color-coding allows you to home in on those most important to-dos.

As you work, take a look at your to-do list regularly—every hour or so. Is it still manageable? Do some tasks need to be reprioritized or rescheduled? If you engage in this review every hour, you will start to take better control of your time. And you will get more work done.

Consider rewarding yourself for your efforts, too. When you cross three tasks off your list, give yourself a break or launch into an easy task next. The sense of accomplishment and reward will keep you motivated.

By taking the time to understand your goals and how you spend your time, and then prioritizing and assigning times to your work, you can create daily to-do lists that are realistic and that ensure you'll get the right work done at the right time. Next, you need to improve how you actually go about working by finding your focus and developing good habits.

Find Your Focus

Find Your Focus

You've set your goals and priorities. Your to-do list is ready. We'll now turn to organizing your environment—both physically and virtually—so that you can become more focused once you begin tackling each task. We'll also look at how you think about your day, finding routines that can minimize the daily decisions you need to make and maximize the energy you have available for important work.

Organize your space

If you can't find your to-do list on your desk—it's buried under your breakfast, hidden under a mountain of paperwork, or scribbled on the back of your child's soccer schedule—chances are you're not going to check off too many items. It's important that the physical space you are working in is conducive to getting work done. Here is how to create a calmer, more efficient work environment:

1. *Eliminate the clutter.* As you begin each item on your to-do list, take the time to file or throw away anything that is not relevant to the task at hand. A clear space allows you the physical and mental capacity to work and eliminates distractions that can lure you off course.

2. *Keep what you need within reach.* If you use a stapler once a month, put it in a drawer. If you use a particular workbook or reference book daily, keep it next to your keyboard. If an item on your desk hasn't been used by the end of the week, file it or throw it away.

3. *Bundle complementary supplies.* Store the staples next to the stapler and the tape refills with the tape dispenser. You'll save the time it takes to hunt for these items later.

4. *Keep a physical inbox.* Clear your chair of any paper, packets, and handwritten notes your coworkers leave you when you're away from your desk. Instead, create an inbox on your desk and direct colleagues to put important documents there. Go through this inbox at the end of each day, readying it for the next. Otherwise, it becomes just another box of clutter.

5. *Make yourself comfortable.* Is your office chair and computer monitor at a comfortable height for you? Is your space aesthetically pleasing? You spend a lot of time in your workspace, so organize it in a way that is comfortable for you.

After you've made some of these changes, check back in with yourself and reassess your environment after a week or so. Is your space working for you? Are you constantly hunting for that notepad you moved? Are you leaving pens everywhere because the coffee mug that holds them is now out of reach? Make the adjustments your space needs to ensure you're comfortable and your space is efficient.

Organize your e-mail

E-mail has brought a number of benefits to the workplace. You're always accessible—to your boss, to colleagues, to customers, and to your loved ones—and it affords you the opportunity to work remotely, to collaborate with thought leaders worldwide, and to work more quickly.

But e-mail can also be a huge disadvantage when it comes to effective work. The constant pinging of incoming messages and an overflowing inbox can be a big distraction, and it can take a lot of time just to sort through and remove unimportant messages.

Just as you took the time to clean up your physical space, take the time to revisit your virtual space:

1. *Clean up that inbox.* Sorting your e-mails by sender will help you delete the backlog of messages you no longer need and the ones you have already responded to.

2. *Create three folders: follow-up, hold, and archive.* For the remainder of your messages, an efficient filing system works online just as it does in your physical office. Create three folders in which you'll place all the e-mails that now remain in your inbox: *follow-up*, where you'll file the messages you need more than a few minutes to respond to; *hold*, for messages that refer to an event in the future, like an invitation; and *archive*, for those messages

you've responded to but want to keep a record of. Going forward, move each message you receive into one of these folders.

3. *Start over.* If you don't have time now to go through all of the messages in your inbox, don't. Instead, create an archive folder and label it "old e-mails." Dump all of your e-mails there and start fresh with a new inbox. Then, as you have time, go into that archived folder and start deleting and organizing. You won't lose any messages you might need later, and you can start organizing incoming messages appropriately.

If you've tried each of these steps and you still need help to manage e-mail overload, try a task manager within your e-mail application. These systems work with your e-mail and allow you to separate the tasks from the messages, so those messages prompting you to do something no longer clog up your inbox. You can also try a separate task manager; there are many options available for Mac and PC users alike.

Organizing your physical and digital workspace helps you work more efficiently by allowing you to focus more effectively on the task at hand and to find items that you're looking for more quickly.

Develop smart routines

You've organized your task list and your space; think next about how you're going through your day. Are you getting bogged down by small decisions like what to wear, when to check e-mail, and where to eat lunch? In order to focus your attention and energy on the work that matters, apply a repeatable structure to your day. Create regular routines and habits.

The more decisions you have to make in a day, the more drained you will feel. Routine helps limit the number of choices you have to make, preserving your energy for actual work. By putting some of your decisions on autopilot, you'll be better equipped when faced with more challenging choices.

Start by identifying what work patterns you may already have in place. For example, you may already start your day by checking e-mail and voice mail, and responding to those messages that are most important before moving on to other tasks. Perhaps you also take the time just after lunch every day to read industry news. Identifying what routines you already have will help you identify what's working and what might not be, so you can adjust accordingly. For example, you may discover that reading those industry headlines after lunch distracts you from work for the rest of the afternoon; you may need to wait until the end of the day to catch up on daily events.

If you find that you don't yet have a routine—or that you want to add to those that are already working for you—consider these suggestions:

- *Begin your day early.* Instead of proclaiming that you're not a morning person, give it a try. For some, early is 5 a.m., when the kids are still asleep and the office is still quiet. In some corporate offices with flexible scheduling, early might be 9 a.m. if everyone else in your group arrives at 10 a.m. Talk to your manager to see if it's possible to adjust your hours so you can get an early start. No matter the time you choose, you'll feel energized by how much more you can check off of your to-do list before noon if you start earlier.

- *Start with yourself.* Take a moment at the start of your day, before you dive into that to-do list, to pause and mark the moment. This gives you an opportunity to appreciate and focus on what you're about to do.

- *Work in 90-minute increments.* Concentrate on one task (or one group of tasks), uninterrupted, for 90 minutes. This is the optimal amount of time for focus. Then, take a break to refuel before switching to your next task.

- *Review your day.* At the end of the day, when you're powering down, review your to-do list. Did you get everything accomplished? Were your expectations realistic? Engaging in this review every day will help you determine where you are assigning time and tasks appropriately, and where your allocations might need refining.

Now, take it a step further. Create additional rituals outside of the office:

- *Get a good night's sleep.* Set a regular bedtime to ensure that you get the same amount of sleep every night. You'll arrive at the office well rested and ready to work.

- *Plan your meals and wardrobe.* As with planning how to spend your time, if you decide every day what you're going to wear, eat for breakfast, and eat for lunch, you may be unnecessarily sapping your energy resources. If you organize your wardrobe into outfits, eat the same foods regularly, and have everything prepared ahead of time, you will be better equipped when hit with decisions that require more thought.

By reorganizing your space and restructuring your day and other choices, you create a work environment that will give you more energy to do the things that matter most. The next step is to keep that focus despite interruptions and other distractions, which we'll cover in the next chapter.

Keep Up the Good Habits

Keep Up the Good Habits

You've prioritized. You've organized. You've identified daily practices to keep yourself working effectively. But you can still veer off course if you're not careful.

To maintain your focus, you need to understand why you get distracted. Identifying what's leading you astray will help you maintain better control of your attention.

Stop procrastinating

You might occasionally invite distractions because there's a task you simply don't want to tackle. But avoidance doesn't get work done. It's important to understand what is behind the impulse to procrastinate so that you can fend it off when it strikes.

The inclination to procrastinate can come from having too much on your plate (the more you have to do, the stronger the inclination to bury your head in the sand and put it off). It can also come from disliking a particular task or not knowing how to do it or where to start. Figure out which of these it is. Answering honestly will help you determine next steps; either get it over with or ask for help from a colleague or manager.

Here are three tips to get yourself focused on the task at hand, even when you just don't want to:

- *Set deadlines for yourself in advance.* Resist the urge to pull an all-nighter. What might have gotten you by in college will not suffice in the workplace. As you've already learned, slotting tasks (and subtasks) into your calendar will help you control your inclination to save everything until the last minute. By seeing these items on your calendar, you'll feel responsible to complete each task in a particular time frame, and you'll gain a sense of accomplishment every time you complete one.

- *Reward yourself.* Take a coffee break or go talk to a colleague once you've finished a particularly dreaded task. Or force yourself to leave a task that you *do* like until after you've finished the one you don't. On days that you just can't seem to focus, consider paying yourself a dollar for each task you accomplish and use the money to buy something you've been wanting. The promise of the reward can help kick-start your motivation.

- *Get help.* If the problem at the outset is that you don't know how to start the project, work with a colleague who can help you. Not only

does working with someone else get you un-
stuck, but it also holds you accountable. Not
wanting to let your colleague down will pro-
pel you forward. You may also discover that it
makes the task more fun.

If you've tried these tactics and you still can't get
started, it may be that you're afraid of the inherent
risk in the project at hand. In getting work done there
is the possibility of failure. But you won't accomplish
anything unless you get started. (See the sidebar "The
Dos and Don'ts of Procrastination.")

Avoid interruptions

Sometimes your work gets put off not by your lack
of motivation, but by outside influences. When you
switch back and forth between to-do items, between a task and an e-mail, or between a task and a

THE DOS AND DON'TS OF PROCRASTINATION

Do:

- Identify the tasks you are likely to put off ahead of time.

- Understand why you've put off a certain task.

- Use deadlines to motivate yourself.

- Reward yourself as you achieve your goals.

Don't:

- Label yourself a procrastinator.

- Extend your deadlines, just for the sake of it.

- Tackle the hard stuff alone.

question from your boss, it takes cognitive energy and time to get back on track to complete the project at hand. It also hinders creativity: You lose great ideas before they have a chance to grow. When you are interrupted, you cannot reflect holistically on your work—what you could do better or differently. Interruption also induces stress. But perhaps the most insidious danger of interruption is that if you stop each task to respond to every incoming e-mail message, you're likely putting mundane work above more crucial work.

There are many external factors that can distract you from your work. E-mail is one—think about how you react every time you hear the ding alerting you to a new message—as is the tendency to multitask. (We discuss both in more detail later.) Another is visits from colleagues: You may want to tell them when you're available for office hours when you're facing an imminent deadline.

Of course, there will be times when a new task, goal, or problem takes priority over what you're currently doing. When this happens, don't shift gears too fast; take a brief break to let your mind and body know you're moving on to something else. Get up from your chair, take a walk, or do some stretches. These actions signal to your brain that something new is about to happen. And you can get back to your previous task after you've conquered this new request.

Don't let e-mail take over

E-mail can be a big culprit when it comes to interruption and loss of productivity. You've already organized your inbox, which should help you focus on the messages that are crucial to tackle, but it's important to carefully manage the time you spend on messages as they come in, when you're supposed to be working on something else. Here are some tips to avoid being distracted by incoming e-mails:

- *Turn it off.* If your e-mail is off, you won't instinctively react to each new message as it comes in. Instead, schedule time every two to three hours to review your e-mails. If that doesn't seem frequent enough, review your inbox every hour on the hour. If you need to, put a note in your e-mail signature telling those you correspond with what times you check e-mail and to call you if something urgent arises.

- *Give it two minutes.* Once you are looking at your inbox, if you can answer an e-mail in two minutes, do it. Don't file it, don't leave it in your inbox to review later, but respond right away. If it requires more than two minutes, schedule a time to reply to it and add it to your to-do list.

- *Rethink "Reply all."* If you're stuck in an e-mail chain with 10 coworkers, consider whether e-mail is the most efficient use of everyone's time. Instead, schedule a quick meeting so that everyone can contribute and get their questions

answered without pulling you away from your
work again and again.

- *Stop unnecessary responses.* You don't need
to close every loop. While a quick "will do" or
"thank you" sounds helpful (and polite), send-
ing e-mails like these throughout the day can
add up to a lot of time wasted. Before you draft
that e-mail, ask yourself if it's helpful. If it's not,
go back to what you were working on.

- *Auto-organize.* Create filters to automatically file or archive regular e-mails that you
may need at some point but distract you from
your work, so you can look at them later (company bulletins, reservation confirmations, or
other automated alerts). Or automatically file
e-mails regarding a specific project so you can
look at them all together, when it's convenient.
And unsubscribe from any newsletters that

you never read that distract from important messages.

Stop multitasking

Multitasking is just like interrupting yourself, continuously. You can't give your work your full attention if you're trying to do everything at once. Here are three myths about multitasking:

Myth 1. Humans are capable of doing two things at once. We're not. So if you are flipping through this book while talking on the phone, put the phone down and read it again. You can only do one thing at a time.

Myth 2. Multitasking makes you more efficient. Wrong. In fact, research shows that it will take you 25% longer to finish the initial task once you've picked up another one.

Myth 3. The stress of multitasking boosts your performance. Anxiety reduces your ability to think clearly or creatively; it also makes you act impulsively. That's not the way you want to operate in the workplace.

Given the constant demands on your time and attention, it's no surprise that interruptions can steal your focus from the work you should be doing. But in your zeal to keep your head down, don't forget to take a step back and recharge. Working too much can be damaging to your focus as well.

Work less

You can't operate at a level of peak performance all the time. People perform best when they alternate between times of intense work and times of rest. Demanding a little less of yourself actually helps you to be more productive, focused, and engaged. Here are two ways to try to put *less* pressure on yourself:

- *Reclaim your lunch hour.* Get out of your office. Take a walk or use the time to exercise.

Have lunch with a friend or colleague. You will be more focused and fueled to perform at your best for the rest of the day. If you can't get out of the office, take 20 minutes to close your door, shut your eyes, and meditate at your desk. Grab your headphones and listen to soothing music or a podcast to help set the tone for relaxation. You may even want to take a brief nap.

- *Take time to think creatively.* Set aside time during your day for brainstorming—with colleagues or alone. Brainstorming often goes to the bottom of your to-do list and rarely gets the time it deserves. Not only is this time rewarding for you, creatively, it can also lead to big ideas for your company.

So far, you've learned what you can do yourself to become more organized and get work done. Now it's time to add another variable into the mix—your colleagues. How do you work more efficiently with those around you?

Work Effectively with Others

Work Effectively with Others

Working productively doesn't always mean working alone. You'll often need to work with others, and for good reason: The people around you can be great resources in helping you get work done. Recognize when it's appropriate to delegate work and learn to do it well; also identify when to ask for help.

Working with others can also slow you down, however. In a social environment like a workplace, you're often driven to do work that you don't need to simply because a colleague asked. You need to learn to recognize when work doesn't add value and know how to say no. Working with your colleagues also often means a lot of meetings; to be efficient, you need to learn to make the most of those gatherings so they don't proliferate. And in today's world of telecommuting and far-flung global offices, it's critical to learn how to work effectively with a virtual team to avoid miscommunication and inefficiency.

Learn to say no

You want to be known as a helpful, eager team player, but you should have a method of assessing the mountain of requests that come your way, especially if you feel as if you're losing sight of your goals and priorities because you're already being pulled in too many directions.

When a colleague asks you for a favor or to take on a new task, consider the following:

1. How valuable is this work to the company? Does it contribute to the company's overall objectives or to the objectives of your team or division? If the work doesn't add value and it's

not having a positive impact on the company's goals, it may not make sense for you to take it on.

2. How important is this activity to your own professional performance goals? Classify the work as essential, important, discretionary, or unimportant. If it's not important to your organization or to the metrics for success that you and your manager have set for you, don't do it.

3. Do you get personal value from this work? Do you enjoy it or do you dislike it altogether? If the work isn't meaningful to you, chances are you're not going to perform the task well and it might not be something worth putting on your list.

4. Do you have enough time to do the work? Even if it's valuable, if you have other high-priority work on your plate, it may not make sense for you to take on this project now.

5. Is this something only you can do because you have a particular skill set or expertise, or could it be accomplished successfully by someone else? If it is the latter, this task is one you should delegate.

Even if the request is coming from your boss, it's acceptable to push back and ask these questions. If you've clearly outlined your tasks and goals, the two of you together will be able to see if this request doesn't fit.

Sometimes the best thing you can do for yourself, and for the business, is to not take on those tasks that add little value and instead commit yourself to the work that matters.

Delegate

Do you find that you're still working in the office every night after everyone else has gone home? Do you feel as if nothing could ever get done without you? Do other people keep offering to help you? If you've answered yes to any of these questions, think about whether you have too much on your plate. You may need to seek help to get work done.

While it's true that there are only so many hours in a day, it's also true that you can free up more of those hours if you delegate (or eliminate) the less important tasks on your list. You're not shirking your responsibilities; you're working efficiently to get the real work of the business done.

What tasks could be done well by someone else? Delegate that work to a colleague or direct report. Here are the three important steps for delegating effectively:

1. *Identify low-value tasks.* Go through your to-do list and look for tasks that are not a high priority for you or your company (like those you identified earlier in the book). Those are

the ones that you should consider delegating. If you're not sure what is within your right to delegate, talk to your manager.

2. *Choose the right person.* Consider what work could best be done by your direct reports, each member of your team, and other colleagues around you. Is there something on your list that would give another team member valuable experience? Is there work that could augment—or take advantage of—a colleague's skill set? Making the work you delegate a part of someone's development goals will ensure the work gets done. For administrative tasks, identify more junior team members who may have more time to do them. Again, work with your manager to make sure that the person you've picked for the handoff makes sense.

3. *Walk away.* The key to successful delegation is to hand off the work and let others deter-

mine how to get it done. Show that you trust your direct reports or colleagues by not intervening or micromanaging the work they're doing. Instead, monitor their progress at a distance and be available for support as they hit roadblocks that might require your expertise.

Once you've delegated some of your work, decide how you will reallocate the time you've freed up: List the two to three things that you would like to be doing but haven't had the time to do. Treat these items as you would others on your to-do list by following the processes described earlier in this book.

You've kept your boss informed throughout this process, but in order to commit to freeing up more time for what's really important, share your time-reallocation plan with her in detail by asking her to review and assess what you've delegated and what you've committed to spending time on. Request that she hold you accountable. If you don't, you're likely to lean on bad habits when you get busy again.

Remember that it takes time to learn how to delegate well. Give yourself that time and know that you will make mistakes. Ask your manager and your colleagues for feedback, so you can adjust for the next time. (See the sidebar "The Dos and Don'ts of Delegation.")

Ask for help

Sometimes it's difficult to admit that you don't know how to do something. But it's worse when your insecurity leads to work getting done incorrectly or a project spiraling out of control. Sometimes you need to reach out to others for assistance.

In some cases, it may be easy to identify who you can ask for help. Remember that person you consulted to see how long a task would take when you were assigning deadlines? Reach out to him again if you're having trouble with that task now that you've

THE DOS AND DON'TS OF DELEGATION

Do:

- Be aware of how much you're working, compared to your colleagues.

- Hand off the tasks that do not fit into your goals and might be best done by somebody else.

- Involve your manager by explaining your delegation plan in detail.

Don't:

- Give someone a task and micromanage how she accomplishes it.

- Assume you're the only one who can get a task done.

- Think you're going to get delegation right every time.

started. If you're just not sure whom to ask, talk to your manager.

Once you know whom to approach, think about how you'll ask for help. Taking more of the initiative will mean that you'll get quicker, better answers.

1. *Start with what you know.* Give the person the information that you have, so that he knows where you're starting from. In addition to giving him important background information that he needs to help you, this will also help you feel more confident.

2. *Have an opinion.* You might not know the right answer, but you should know where you'd like to begin or have a suggested course of action. Explain to the other person the direction you'd like to take and let him give you input on whether or not he thinks it's the right one, rather than making him come up with a plan himself (that will take a lot more time

and effort on his part than reacting to your ideas).

3. *Be direct.* There will be times when you ask for help and you still don't understand the direction you're given. Ask again. The person who is assisting you won't know if his instructions are helpful if you aren't clear with him.

Interacting with others efficiently can be a great asset as you work toward your goals. But you won't always be working one on one with your coworkers. Now let's look at how you can be more productive when you're leading a meeting with a group.

Make meetings more productive

Whether the purpose of your meeting is to bring people together to make a decision (or several decisions), to brainstorm, to give status reports, or to share other information, gatherings of multiple people can become inefficient very quickly. Here's how to make your time together more productive:

- *Get the right people together.* If the vice president of marketing is out of the office and you can't make the decision without her, reschedule the meeting. Otherwise you're wasting time for yourself and everyone else.

- *Set an agenda.* Outline what will be covered in the meeting in advance and route that agenda to the attendees ahead of time, along with any other important documents needed for the meeting. Two to three days in advance of the meeting is ideal to give attendees a chance to review. Label each agenda item as "for discussion," "for information," or "for decision," so that everyone in the room is clear on what the action items are during the meeting. Gathering to meet when participants are unaware of what you'll be discussing and haven't prepared is likely to waste everyone's time as well.

- *Assign time slots for each agenda item.* This will help ensure that you don't spend more time than necessary—or than you have available—on any one agenda item. Begin with the most important to-dos, too, since most people come to a meeting with energy and enthusiasm that will decrease as the meeting progresses.

- *Stick to the 90-minute rule.* Very few things are accomplished after 90 minutes. If it's not possible to cover everything you need to in that time frame, schedule a follow-up meeting rather than taking the time all in one session. Your time together will be more productive.

Running effective meetings will improve the way you work—and also the way your colleagues work. They will appreciate your respect of their time and, ideally, learn from your own good habits, making other meetings you attend more efficient as well.

Make virtual work more effective

Many employees work from home or from another location outside of a company's main headquarters. Whether it's because of the company's far-flung global offices or as the result of a flexible work benefit, working off-site has become a normal part of our work lives.

Virtual work demands that you communicate clearly or you're going to be spending a lot of time resolving misunderstandings or redoing work. There's a lot of room for confusion when you're not addressing your colleagues face-to-face. Often, you can't see the person you're talking to. Social cues and the information we get by looking someone in the eye—and seeing her in her environment—are gone. Tone can be misread. You have to work harder to ensure you're understood.

If you're part of a virtual team, establish communication norms. For instance, how long will it take you to respond to e-mail? Will all team calls take place via Skype or through some other type of videoconferencing? If a team member needs to be reached right away, does she prefer a phone call to an e-mail? When these norms are made clear at the outset, you won't need to have a back-and-forth before a meeting; you'll already know that you'll be using a set videoconference line. Nor will you need to flood your colleague's inbox with messages asking for a response to an e-mail you sent 20 minutes ago. You'll know he'll be in touch within the hour, and you can devote the time before you hear from him to other important work.

Keep the following tips in mind to make sure that your communications are understood and efficient.

- *Spell it out.* Be clear and specific in your messages. More communication is better than less. If you're unsure whether your message was clear, ask your colleagues to paraphrase it for you; if they don't get it quite right, clarify it again. For example, if you need a response by a particular date, communicate that deadline explicitly. Saying, "I look forward to hearing back from you," doesn't sound urgent, and it's unclear when you'll need a response. Instead, be specific: "I need your feedback by end of day Thursday so I can communicate it to the client during our call on Friday morning."

- *Respond promptly.* In virtual work, you don't have the benefit of knowing where your colleagues are or what they've been doing all day. If a virtual colleague sends you an e-mail, he may not know that you've been stuck in a conference room for hours, or that you've been working on a specific project and have turned off your e-mail alerts; he may assume that your lack of response means that his request isn't important to you. Let your virtual teammates know when you might be unavailable and respond to their e-mails as quickly as possible, even if that response is a brief one to tell them you aren't available at the moment but will be back in touch soon. They will spend less time trying to track you down, and you can feel less stressed to respond to them as soon as you do get out of your meeting or step away from your project.

If you're the one working away from a central office, remember that virtual work requires the same commitment to task and routine as any other kind of work; don't let your new and improved productivity habits lapse when you or others are out of the room. All of the great work you've done to be productive, and to work well with others, is even more critical when you aren't always working face-to-face.

Assess Your Progress

Assess Your Progress

All of these to-do lists, organization tools, and routines aren't worth the effort if they aren't helping to make you more efficient. Take the time every few months—or at least once a year—to ask yourself whether they are working and whether you've come closer to achieving the personal and professional goals you set earlier in the book.

Reflect and adjust

During this period of review, revisit the goals you outlined in the beginning of "Identify What Needs to Get

Done" and ask yourself if you're now on track to meet them. If there's still room for improvement, examine which tools are contributing to your productivity and which aren't.

Are you using your to-do lists, or do you only look at the tasks that you've entered into your online calendar? Are you missing important, urgent communication with your teammates because you're checking e-mail too infrequently? If you're finding that a particular tool or routine isn't useful, modify or jettison it. You aren't committed to the approaches you try; the point is to find what works for you.

Things also get messy even after they've been organized. Make time—every four to six months—to reset. Go through your filing system, your e-mails, and your to-do lists, and make sure everything is still getting sorted according to the method you devised at the outset. It feels good to clean things up regularly and give yourself a fresh start.

Look at the small successes you've had, even if they don't appear on a financial chart. These indicate that some change you've made to your way of working has improved your productivity. For example, it's OK if your inbox now has a dozen messages in it, instead of the zero it had when you first set up your folders and filters. Remember four months ago when you had over two hundred messages? This is real progress! Identify where your organizational system is working, and if you need to make small adjustments, allow yourself some variance.

Finally, anticipate obsolescence. Productivity tools and systems will come and go, especially the digital ones. And just as technology changes, so too might your preferences. Understand and prepare for this by using software tools that allow you to export your data so that you're not stuck in any one platform. Or know that you might migrate from a paper to-do list to an online list, or vice versa. These kinds of changes are fine, as long as they are helping you get work done.

Remember, this is not a one-size-fits-all process. Apply your own creativity and make sure your system works for you. Embrace the fact that you operate in a certain way, and that certain things work for you that may not work for others. Perhaps you like to review your organizational plan as part of "spring cleaning," or maybe you like to reorganize every January 1 because it recharges you. Whatever system works for you is fine; the important thing is to have a system and review it over time.

Taking the time to step back and reconfigure how you work is critical to improving your productivity. But it's not a one-time process: Being prepared for challenges to your focus and to the positive habits you've begun to build will keep you productive—and improve your work and that of the colleagues with whom you collaborate. Establishing processes for identifying and scheduling your most important tasks and implementing changes that result in greater focus and efficiency are just the first steps. By checking in on these processes and adjusting them frequently, you will enjoy not only a more effective way to get work done, but ideally a more productive way to live.

Learn More

Books

Allen, David. *Getting Things Done: The Art of Stress-Free Productivity*. New York: Penguin Group, 2001.

Veteran coach and management consultant David Allen shares his methods for stress-free performance based on the notion that our productivity is directly proportional to our ability to relax. This classic in the genre shows readers how to apply the "do it, delegate it, defer it, drop it" rule to empty e-mail inboxes, reassess goals, stay focused, plan projects, and overcome feelings of confusion and anxiety.

Halvorson, Heidi Grant. *9 Things Successful People Do Differently*. Boston: Harvard Business Review Press, 2012.

According to author Heidi Grant Halvorson, accomplished people reach their goals because of what they do, not just who they are. In this short, practical, research-based book, she explains exactly what strategies have the biggest impact on performance, including setting specific goals, using if-then planning, and monitoring your progress.

Harvard Business School Publishing. *HBR Guide to Getting the Right Work Done*. Boston: Harvard Business Review Press, 2012.

This guide takes a deeper dive into productivity tactics than this 20-Minute Manager does with additional practical how-tos and sample routines. Topics include prioritizing your work, determining what work is urgent, delegating effectively, renewing your energy, and developing good work habits.

Harvard Business School Publishing. *Managing Time*. Boston: Harvard Business Review Press, 2014.

While *Getting Work Done* walks through some of the basics of time management as well as other productivity tips and tricks, *Managing Time* focuses more deeply on the tried-and-true methods of managing your time and schedule. In addition to what's included in this book, readers will learn, for example, how to get a derailed schedule back on track and how to re-allocate time to reflect their goals.

Samuel, Alexandra. *Work Smarter, Rule Your Email*. Boston: Harvard Business Review Press, 2014.

By reducing the amount of time spent on e-mail, Alexandra Samuel argues, readers can focus their time and attention on the work that matters most. Using an e-mail program's already existing filtering tools can do the heavy lifting in managing an overflowing inbox. This short ebook explains how to set them up.

Articles and Periodicals

Birkinshaw, Julian, and Jordan Cohen. "Make Time for the Work That Matters." *Harvard Business Review*, September 2013 (product #R1309K).

This article reveals an exercise designed to help readers make small but significant changes to their day-to-day work schedules in order to boost productivity.

"Find Your Focus: Get Things Done the Smart Way." HBR *OnPoint*, November 2013 (product #OPWI13).

This issue of HBR *OnPoint* helps readers think about and manage their time in order to maximize both productivity and effectiveness.

Pozen, Robert C. "Managing Yourself: Extreme Productivity." *Harvard Business Review*, May 2011 (product #R1105K).

In this article, Harvard Business School senior lecturer Robert Pozen presents six principles and practices to maximize personal productivity without sacrificing health or family life, distilled from his blog posts on HBR.org.

Online Resources

"Boost Your Productivity with Microbreaks." HBR.org Ideacast. April 5, 2012. http://blogs.hbr.org/2012/04/boost-your -productivity-with-m/.

According to research, taking breaks can help your productivity, if they are the right breaks. This interview with Charlotte Fritz, professor at Portland State University, defines for listeners which breaks can energize you and which ones leave you disengaged.

"Develop Productivity Rituals." HBR.org Video. January 3, 2012. http://blogs.hbr.org/2012/01/develop-productivity -rituals/.

Tony Schwartz, president and CEO of The Energy Project, lists the top-four habits that help him get more work done, using insights gleaned from others who manage to get things done while still having a life. His secret? Develop rituals.

"Find Time to Achieve Your Vision." HBR.org Slideshow. http://hbr.org/web/slideshows/find-time-to-achieve-your -vision/1-slide.

This slideshow, based on Robert Steven Kaplan's *What to Ask the Person in the Mirror: Critical Questions for Becoming a More Effective Leader and Reaching Your Potential*, suggests a process to help readers focus on their priorities by asking themselves key questions.

Sources

General Sources

Bielaszka-DuVernay, Christina. "The Dangers of Distraction." HBR.org, January 19, 2009. http://blogs.hbr.org/2009/01/pay-attention-an-interview-wit/.

DeLong, Thomas J. *Flying Without a Net: Turn Fear of Change into Fuel for Success*. Boston: Harvard Business Review Press, 2011.

DeMaio, Steven. "How to Train Your Pet Peeve." HBR.org, October 5, 2009. http://blogs.hbr.org/2009/10/how-to-train-your-pet-peeve/.

Dutta, Soumitra. "What's Your Personal Social Media Strategy?" *Harvard Business Review*, November 2010 (product #R1011L).

"Find Time to Achieve Your Vision." HBR.org Slideshow. http://hbr.org/web/slideshows/find-time-to-achieve-your-vision/1-slide.

"Find Your Focus: Get Things Done the Smart Way." HBR *OnPoint*. November 2013 (product #OPWI13).

Goleman, Daniel. "What Makes a Leader?" *Harvard Business Review*, January 2004 (product #R0401H).

Sources

Goleman, Daniel, Richard Boyatzis, and Annie McKee. *Primal Leadership: The Hidden Driver of Great Performance*. Boston: Harvard Business Review Press, 2013.

Groysberg, Boris, and Robin Abrahams. "Manage Your Work, Manage Your Life." *Harvard Business Review*, March 2014 (product #R1403C).

Hammerness, Paul, MD, and Margaret Moore. "Train Your Brain to Focus." HBR.org, January 18, 2012. http://blogs .hbr.org/2012/01/train-your-brain-to-focus/.

Harvard Business School Publishing. *HBR Guide to Getting the Right Work Done*. Boston: Harvard Business Review Press, 2012.

Harvard Business School Publishing. *Managing Time*. Boston: Harvard Business Review Press, 2014.

Kaplan, Robert Steven. *What to Ask the Person in the Mirror: Critical Questions for Becoming a More Effective Leader and Reaching Your Potential*. Boston: Harvard Business Review Press, 2011.

Katz, Robert L. "Skills of an Effective Administrator." *Harvard Business Review*, September 1974 (product #74509).

McGinn, Daniel. "Being More Productive." *Harvard Business Review*, May 2011 (product #R1105D).

Pozen, Robert C., and Justin Fox. "Pozen on Personal Productivity." HBR.org, March 14, 2011. http://blogs.hbr.org/ 2011/03/pozen-personal-productivity/.

Samuel, Alexandra. "Stop Using Your Inbox as a To-Do List." HBR.org, March 7, 2014. http://blogs.hbr.org/ 2014/03/stop-using-your-inbox-as-a-to-do-list/.

Samuel, Alexandra. *Work Smarter, Rule Your Email*. Boston: Harvard Business Review Press, 2014.

Schwartz, Tony. "The Productivity Paradox: How Sony Pictures Gets More Out of People by Demanding Less." *Harvard Business Review*, June 2010 (product #R1006C).

"Test Yourself: Are You Headed for an Energy Crisis?" HBR.org Assessment. http://hbr.org/web/tools/2008/12/manage-energy-not-time.

"Vision Statement: The Multitasking Paradox." *Harvard Business Review*, March 2013 (product #F1303Z).

Additional Chapter-by-Chapter Sources

Why Invest Time in Improving Your Productivity?

David, Susan. "Don't Sabotage Yourself." HBR.org, May 29, 2012. http://blogs.hbr.org/2012/05/dont-sabotage-yourself/.

Identify What Needs to Get Done

Drucker, Peter. *Managing Oneself*. Boston: Harvard Business School Press, 2008.

Ghoshal, Sumantra, and Heike Bruch. "Reclaim Your Job." *Harvard Business Review*, March 2004 (product #R0403B).

Sources

Samuel, Alexandra. "A 7-Step Process to Achieving Your Goals." HBR.org, January 6, 2012. http://blogs.hbr.org/2012/01/the-7-step-process-to-achieving-your-goals/.

Schedule Your Work

Bregman, Peter. "A Better Way to Manage Your To-Do List." HBR.org, February 24, 2011. http://blogs.hbr.org/2011/02/a-better-way-to-manage-your-to/.

Bregman, Peter. "What to Do With Your To-Do List." HBR.org, March 2, 2011. http://blogs.hbr.org/2011/03/what-to-do-with-your-to-do-lis/.

Carr, Nicholas G. "Curbing the Procrastination Instinct." *Harvard Business Review*, October 2001 (product #F0109C).

Halvorson, Heidi Grant. "Here's What Really Happens When You Extend a Deadline." HBR.org, August 19, 2013. http://blogs.hbr.org/2013/08/heres-what-really-happens-when/.

Moore, Don A. "Deadline Pressure: Use It to Your Advantage." *Negotiation*, August 2004 (product #N0408A).

Pratt, George. "Deadlines . . . Get It Done or Get It Done Right?" HBR.org, April 18, 2007. http://blogs.hbr.org/2007/04/deadlinesget-it-done-or-get-it/.

Find Your Focus

"Boost Your Productivity with Social Media." HBR.org Ideacast, December 20, 2012. http://blogs.hbr.org/2012/12/boost-your-productivity-with-s/.

Bregman, Peter. "The Value of Ritual in Your Workday." HBR
.org, December 8, 2010. http://blogs.hbr.org/2010/12/
the-value-of-ritual-in-your-wo/.

DeMaio, Steven. "The Art of the Self-Imposed Deadline."
HBR.org, March 25, 2009. http://blogs.hbr.org/2009/
03/the-art-of-the-selfimposed-dea/.

"Develop Productivity Rituals." HBR.org Video, January 3,
2012. http://blogs.hbr.org/2012/01/develop-productivity
-rituals/.

Pozen, Robert C. "Boring Is Productive." HBR.org, September 19, 2012. http://blogs.hbr.org/2012/09/boring-is
-productive/.

"Rely on Routines to Free Your Mental Energy." *Harvard
Business Review* Management Tip. February 17, 2014.
http://hbr.org/tip/2014/02/17/rely-on-routines-to-free
-your-mental-energy.

Schwartz, Tony. "A 90-Minute Plan for Personal Effectiveness." HBR.org, January 24, 2011. http://blogs.hbr.org/
2011/01/the-most-important-practice-i/.

Schwartz, Tony. "The Only Way to Get Important Things
Done." HBR.org, May 24, 2011. http://blogs.hbr.org/2011/
05/the-only-way-to-get-important/.

Trapani, Gina. "Organize Your Workspace for Maximum Productivity." HBR.org, June 1, 2009. http://blogs.hbr.org/
2009/06/organize-your-workspace-for-ma/.

Keep Up the Good Habits

"Boost Your Productivity with Microbreaks." HBR.org Idea-cast, April 5, 2012. http://blogs.hbr.org/2012/04/boost -your-productivity-with-m/.

Bregman, Peter. "The Unexpected Antidote to Procrastina-tion." HBR.org, May 10, 2013. http://blogs.hbr.org/2013/ 05/the-unexpected-antidote-to-pro/.

Halvorson, Heidi Grant. "How to Make Yourself Work When You Just Don't Want To." HBR.org, February 14, 2014. http://blogs.hbr.org/2014/02/how-to-make-yourself -work-when-you-just-dont-want-to/.

"Reward Yourself by Doing the Tasks You Hate." *Harvard Business Review* Management Tip. November 1, 2012. http://hbr.org/tip/2012/11/01/reward-yourself-for -doing-the-tasks-you-hate.

Schwartz, Tony. "Four Destructive Myths Most Companies Still Live By." HBR.org, November 1, 2011. http://blogs .hbr.org/2011/11/four-destructive-myths-most-co/.

Work Effectively with Others

Birkinshaw, Julian, and Jordan Cohen. "Make Time for the Work That Matters." *Harvard Business Review*, September 2013 (product #R1309K).

Gallo, Amy. "Why Aren't You Delegating?" HBR.org, July 26, 2012. http://blogs.hbr.org/2012/07/why-arent-you -delegating/.

Jay, Antony. "How to Run a Meeting." *Harvard Business Review*, March 1976 (product #76204).

Saunders, Elizabeth Grace. "How Office Control Freaks Can Learn to Let Go." HBR.org, October 23, 2013. http://blogs.hbr.org/2013/10/how-office-control-freaks-can-learn-to-let-go/.

"Three Steps for Asking for Help without Looking Stupid." *Harvard Business Review* Management Tip. January 26, 2010. http://hbr.org/tip/2010/01/26/three-steps-for-asking-for-help-without-looking-stupid.

Index

Index

Notes

Notes

Notes

Notes

Notes

Notes

Notes

Notes

Notes

Smarter than the average guide.

Harvard Business Review Guides

If you enjoyed this book and want more comprehensive guidance on essential professional skills, turn to the **HBR Guides series**. Packed with concise, practical tips from leading experts—and examples that make them easy to apply—these books help you master big work challenges with advice from the most trusted brand in business.

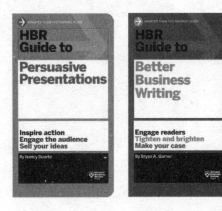